TRIGGER WARNING

TRIGGER WARNING

HARLEY VAUGHN

NEW DEGREE PRESS
COPYRIGHT © 2021 HARLEY VAUGHN
All rights reserved.

TRIGGER WARNING

ISBN   978-1-63676-559-4 *Paperback*
        978-1-63676-140-4 *Kindle Ebook*
        978-1-63676-141-1 *Ebook*

"Harley beautifully combines words to tell stories that others are afraid to tell. She explores emotions and puts words to feelings others haven't. Poetry that is simply inspiring, challenging, and captivating."

— BREANNA DECKER, AUTHOR OF *WEDDING Z: HOW TO REIMAGINE WEDDINGS FOR THE NEXT GENERATION*

"*Trigger Warning* is a courageous and compelling anthology. Harley's poetry will capture your attention and your emotions. I couldn't put it down after I picked it up."

— GRANT DEVER, AUTHOR OF *LEAD THE FUTURE*

"Vaughn's words are a beacon of light that shines through darkness—they give hope where it is needed most. Her words promote healing in a gentle and intimate way."

— LAUREN STIKELEATHER, AUTHOR OF *A MIXING POT OF POEMS FOR THOUGHT*

"Honest and raw, Vaughn's words speak for those who can't in their darkest times and points us all to light."

— JULIA WEIDMAN, AUTHOR OF *I AM GLASS*

"A powerful book of poetry that will make you want to fight depression and win, once and for all."

— AMY DONG, AUTHOR OF *TWENTY-ONE YEARS YOUNG*

"It is lovely—and rare—to find this type of warmth in a book. *Trigger Warning* is the accepting, comforting friend we all wished we had during the darkest times of our lives."

— BAILEE NOELLA, AUTHOR OF *BATHTUB IN FLAMES*.

"From what I've seen from *Trigger Warning*, there's a very obvious and deep connection to the subject matter. Somehow, even when hitting the darker thoughts and emotions, they trigger a sense of hope because you know it's not the end, that someone has been through it and has made it. When I think of *Trigger Warning* and the words that seem to float off the page, I smell rain. The thunderstorms and the quiet after, the violent rain clashing with a more violent sea and the rainbow that comes out of the mist eventually. Overall, beautiful and definitely a favorite."

— JADE WAUGHTEL, PSYCHOLOGY STUDENT, AUBURN UNIVERSITY

"Harley Vaughn's *Trigger Warning* is so beautifully written. Each poem manages to stir up emotions and thoughts that many of us share but aren't quite sure how to express."

— TAMMY DARWIN

"While covering taboo subjects, Vaughn's words are a comfort to those ever touched by any mental health issues, reminding all that we are not alone."

— CASSONDRA NANOFF

"Harley Vaughn's book, *Trigger Warning*, grabs you by the heart and never lets go. You will need tissues. Ms. Vaughn evokes an emotional intensity that I have not felt since reading Sylvia Plath's *The Bell Jar*. The poems in this book put into words the feelings that most of us only wish we had the eloquence, and the guts, to express."

— TERESA LOVELL, FOUNDER OF BIG CAT TECH REPAIR

"*Trigger Warning* paints a vivid image of Vaughn's very personal journey through mental illness. Her words will grip your heart as she gives you a glimpse into her struggles with depression . . . trauma, and overcoming self-harm. Her poems bring to life the emotional turmoil and pain that many people suffer from, and the beauty of loving and finding oneself in a way that is open and vulnerable and real."

— RACHAEL TATE, COUNSELOR AT LILLIAN C. POOLE ELEMENTARY SCHOOL

"*Trigger Warning* does a phenomenal job at giving a voice to the uncomfortable things we don't like to talk about today. The unbridled emotion this collection of poems evokes is unchallenged and raw."

— KERRICK TAGGART

To those I have loved. To those I have lost. There is still a place in my heart, holding all the moments we have shared together.

To the past me, for creating memories, both good and bad. To learning lessons throughout your childhood that have led you here.

To the present me, for being as brave and strong as you are. To keeping your head held high and your feet rooted to the Earth.

To the future me, for I know that you are far in life. To everything that you have accomplished and all you have overcome.

Lastly, a deep gratitude for the special few in my life who have pulled me through the bad times. The few who have provided a listening ear and a shoulder to cry on when I needed it most. The few who have shown me that life is so beautiful and worth living. You are a main factor in my happiness, and I love you all. Thank you for never giving up on me.

*My dark days made me strong. Or maybe
I already was strong, and they made me prove it.*

— EMERY LORD, *WHEN WE COLLIDED*

CONTENTS

I.	NOTE FROM THE AUTHOR	15
II.	INTRODUCTION	17
III.	LOVE	21
IV.	LOSS	33
V.	BATTLES	51
VI.	RECOVERY	87
VII.	HOTLINES	107
VIII.	ACKNOWLEDGEMENTS	111
IX.	APPENDIX	113

NOTE FROM THE AUTHOR

You are not alone.

Everyone goes through something terrible in their life, whether it is something deemed small or traumatic. We all have dark times, and we often forget that we are not the only ones to experience these things. Perhaps it is just human nature to believe that we are alone, full of error or fault—like each one of us are on our own out of eight billion people with something going on. That is completely incorrect.

Maybe you personally experienced something traumatic. Studies from the Substance Abuse and Mental Health Services Administration indicate that *"61% of men and 51% of women report at least one traumatic event in their lifetimes."*[1]

Maybe your case is not as extreme. Maybe you just have depression, which *"affects [about] one in 15 adults (6.7%) in any given year,"* but you feel guilty because you "don't have a reason to be depressed." Situations like this cause people to feel like they are ungrateful because nothing big is there to "justify" their sadness.[2]

---

1 "Statistics on Mental Trauma," FHE Health, accessed on October 26, 2020.
2 "What is Depression?" Felix Torres, American Psychiatric Association, accessed on October 26, 2020.

With so much happening, all of us have something. It could have been a death, an assault, or something that is unique and "uncommon" to go through. For example, some people witness deaths or are victims of physical or sexual assault. These are cases where it is harder to open up to people, and when you do, you're probably the only person of your peers to have experienced it. A situation like this causes the sense of "no one knows what I am going through."

Please hear me when I tell you that your problems are not insignificant compared to those around you.

If something affects you and the way you feel, it is okay to be upset. No one can undermine your hurt or take that from you. Own it because it is yours.

Though it feels that you are alone, I promise there are others that have dealt, are dealing, or will deal with what you are going through. Some can empathize and some can only sympathize, but that is okay. That means there is always help. There is always someone who will sit and listen to you, even if they do not have the right words to say to offer comfort. Someone will always hear you calling for help.

If you feel that you cannot express your stories or problems with people around you, I have included various hotlines in the back of this book for you.

Take care of yourself and get the help you deserve because you matter.

Your feelings are valid.

You are not alone, no matter what you deal with.

INTRODUCTION

I could not shake the feeling that I did not matter.

That I was a burden and ungrateful because I had so much and still was not happy.

I felt alone.

Today I know I was not alone.

* * *

Trigger Warning

For years, I personally struggled with depression. I never opened up to anyone about it, because I thought that I had no reason to feel what I was feeling. I put a lid on it and kept going through the motions of the days. Everything in my head was a constant battle between "I hate myself" and "I have no reason to hate myself."

It only got worse as time went on.

My best friend lost her father at a young age, but she always seemed so happy and carefree. This caused me to feel incredibly guilty for feeling the way I did. I had not lost anyone close to me. I did not experience a big life-changing thing that left me hanging.

I could not shake the feeling that I did not matter. That I was a burden and ungrateful because I had so much and still was not happy. I had a roof over my head, loving parents, good health, food on the table, and an overall decent childhood. On top of an average home life, I was excelling in school, had an idea of what I wanted to do when I grew up, and never got into trouble. Nothing really happened to make me question my worth, but in the end I still did. I still was not happy with myself and I never really had a reason not to be content, which almost made me feel worse.

In middle school, I started to hurt myself.

Cutting, burning, hitting myself until I bruised.

By the time I was a sophomore in high school, I had attempted suicide three different times.

* * *

That period of my life was so dark and heavy, and I am not proud of any of it. I knew I needed help and I finally reached out and got it. I would talk to counselors, call hotlines, and journal all my thoughts just to get them all out.

I turned myself around.

I recovered, relapsed a few times, and recovered again.

I am now in college. I lived long enough to see myself graduate and go to a university, and I am so proud of who I am and who I am still becoming.

I got the help I needed and am still getting it. Some days are better than others, but I now know that I matter. I am worth every breath I take and every beat that my heart makes. I learned that I could talk to people—that people will help you up when you have fallen, and they will quickly lend a shoulder to cry on when needed.

I realized that I am not alone.

But not everyone has made it through the darkness and into the light.

* * *

In writing my book, I hope to reach out and indirectly help whoever needs this.

Writing this was a very emotional journey for me, and I am hoping that it will inspire and motivate others to stand up and ask for help. Not only do I want to encourage others to get the support they need, but I also hope to normalize the topics discussed throughout my book and break the stigma. Mental illnesses are not a light subject and should not be brushed off when brought up.

When I went through my heavy years, poetry was something that I discovered helped me cope a lot. At first, I was reading these unrealistic love poems. They were sweet, but I, myself, could not completely relate to love. That is when I discovered slam poetry. These poets were speaking on deep subjects—things I was going through and could actually connect with. Each poem spoke so directly on issues like depression, anxiety, eating disorders, assault, and other hard-hitting topics. They had a way of intriguing me while also normalizing talking about each problem. That was when I knew that I needed to get involved.

This is not to say that happy, lovey-dovey poetry does not aid in people's recovery progress. In fact, I wrote a few of my own to include here because I know that people out there can relate. This is not to say that love poems are not helpful, but to say that poetry written about uncomfortable situations and circumstances can be more comforting to individuals who feel alone in their battles. As humans we rely on validation. I hope that this book gives that to you all and allows you to feel more loved and understood.

LOVE

The Way You Are

Sunday morning sunlight leaks through the
window beside our bed and spills over your face,
turning your dark brown eyes into pools of honey.
I like you like this —
groggy and vulnerable,
peaceful and lovely.

Wednesday evening pancakes sizzle in the cast
iron as our dirty clothes tell the story
of a flour and batter fight, not ten minutes ago.
I like you like this —
silly and relaxed,
childlike and wonderful.

Friday night screams bounce off our thin walls
knocking lamps to the ground like an earthquake,
but neither of us back down from our positions.
I do not like you like this —
stubborn and annoying,
strong and proud.

I love you like this.

A Moment of Respite

Let me breathe you in,
At least until I forget the scent
Of my loneliness.

Realization

You're still the blood in my veins, the marrow in my bones. You're the goosebumps down my spine, the tingling in my fingertips. You've become the echoing in my mind and the beating of my heart. All my breaths and all my thoughts. You're the things I used to hate about myself before you touched them. I've sold my soul to you, Lucifer, but I'm still not good enough to be the dirt under your nails or feel the annoyance of your morning breath. I am but a useless speck in this whole damn universe, but oh my god, you are everything and more. You are ever more beautiful than galaxies beyond lightyears. And I realize, after all this, that I am in love with you.

A Thoughtful Breakup

Maybe one day you will leave me,
But do not take these memories with you.

I want to remember that you
Like your coffee black and my hair down.
I want to remember the way we laughed
When you woke me up at 4 a.m.
Just to bake cookies and
The way your hair fell
Disheveled in your face.
I want to remember when you
First told me that you didn't
Want to wake up without me
Next to you.

Maybe one day you will leave me,
But spare the moments that remind me that
We were once in love.

Love Is Blind

There is something inevitable
About falling in love with someone
Who is predestined to break your heart.
You know the look in their eyes says
"I will ruin you,"
So you close yours
In hopes that going blind
Will change the outcome.

Somewhere Between You and I

Someone somewhere right now is taking their last breath. Someone somewhere right now is taking their first. Right here, right now, I stand in front of you, admiring all your beauty. Your tousled hair and strong arms. Your brown eyes and matching freckles. I am breathless. I stare at you and all the air escapes my lungs. All my words catch in my throat. Tell me, is that me offering breath to the dying or having it stolen by the living?

I Want to Give You Hope, But I Can't

I want to wrap you in sunshine,
Kiss you daffodils.
I want to tell you that this is
Only temporary.
That the rain will pass,
That it will leave a rainbow-paved path.

But I do not know that,
So I will not tell you so.
Instead I will hold your hand,
Brave this storm with you,
And hope that you would do the same
For me.

Modern-Day Cinderella

I fell in love with a girl
Who tasted like cigarettes and cheap lip gloss.
Cherry and Menthol danced on my tongue
For hours on end.
Sometimes I still kiss strangers
Just to find her in other people.

What Can I Do to Help?

Just hold me tight,
And tell me
Everything will be okay—
Even if it won't.

The Big Bang

I want you to tug at the strings of my macrocosm. Pull one until all my planets are out of balance. Jerk them until every star in my galaxies collide, until all the planets undergo a supernova. Yank at each and every little string tied around the very fibers and beings of the infinity that is me. And please, oh please, twitch these tiny ropes until each snap suddenly, causing every bit of cosmos within me to crash down in uncontrollable spirals. And as each one hits the ground, watch my worlds collapse into microscopic pieces. Fragile and broken like I've become. Build me up into an immense form of beauty and then break me. Push me into an incredible explosion and watch as I come back as the universe.

LOSS
___

Addicted to You

I almost texted you this morning.
And then, I remembered that you don't love me anymore,
And messaging you would mean that
I am a recovering addict, relapsing on the thing
That destroys me most.

Do You Hear Me?

I call out your name, but it sounds like
I am reciting a language unknown to my tongue.
It burns with each sharp syllable and lingers like dissolving salt,
Taking its time to remind me of the pain your name carries.

How foreign it is to utter you
Into existence
After I have tried so hard
To erase you from
The corners of my mind.

Lauren

When you left, you forgot your shirt and I couldn't stop wearing it, because it was yours and your lingering smell was so incredibly nostalgic. It was a blend of all the memories we created together. I wore it like a prom queen sash and moped around my house for weeks. I was so broken. After twenty-three days wrapped up in your favorite black shirt and my sadness, I decided to say goodbye and wash it. But as I made up my bed, I couldn't help but inhale your scent again, and realized that it spread into the fabrics of all my clothes and sheets in the wash. Now I am lying in the dark at 3:20 a.m.—I cannot sleep because the smell of you fills my lungs and the thought of you makes me cry. You left and I let you, and that is the stupidest thing anyone can do. But you wanted to go, and I loved you. Who am I to stop you from doing what your free spirit wanted? But maybe if I curl up and just breathe in the sheets, you will somehow come back to me. My head disagrees, but my heart is still skipping beats, trying to mimic the hurried rhythm it once held when you kissed me. I just wish you are happy wherever you are . . . even if it's not with me.

Numb

I can't stop thinking about how things seemed so perfect but are so broken. I've not slept in days, and I wish I could say it's been anything but torture. I feel my heart shattering in my fucking hands. I feel the crystal shards push deeper into my calloused palms — it's the first time I've felt anything but numb in weeks. It is also the first time in weeks that I'm writing, and it's the hardest thing I've ever had to do. Not because I did not used to be sad but because this is about you. I'm sorry, I'm sorry that you had to be another good thing of mine gone wrong. Always the right emotions, but never the right time.

Comparison

Compared to you,
Alcohol is the sweetest thing
There is.
Sweeter than all of the lies
You have ever told me and
I wish I would have
Figured that out before
I kissed your lips
And recoiled from the burn.
But no matter how much I drink,
I can't seem to get drunk enough
To forget you.

The Art of a Heartbreak

Vibrant blue eyes made their way into you and tore you apart. Now you remember that you built these walls to keep yourself safe, untouched by heartbreak. But now, the walls are glittered in his graffiti. Beautiful greens, pinks, and neon yellows. Him, him, him. He refuses to leave your mind and you refuse to let him. Your scattered heart cries out in pain as you swear that you will never love again. How you will never get back the best parts of you because he robbed you of their existence. How he strapped you into a dangerous ride that no one prepared you for, that you never asked to get on. How he ruined you. How you let him.

Why Couldn't I Tell You How I Felt?

But I confidently down the many bottles of alcohol because no matter how badly it burns my throat, it will never hurt as badly as the words I could never say to you. And I so boldly puff every cigarette that will fit in my hand because no matter how much smoke fills my lungs, I'm convinced that it is better for me than yearning to breathe you in again.

2 AM

2:17 a.m.
I remember when you whispered my name in my ear, and I swear it sounded better than my favorite song.

2:23 a.m.
None of my shirts or sweaters feel as good as your arms wrapped around me.

2:24 a.m.
Every night you drank, and I wonder if you were trying to wash away the taste of me?

2:27 a.m.
My sheets and pillows still smell of you.

2:31 a.m.
Fuck.

2:35 a.m.
Lately my hair has always been a mess but not because your hands were tangled in it.

2:39 a.m.
Smoking kills, yet you lit a cigarette at least once when you were out with me. Did being around me make you feel like you wanted to die?

2:41 a.m.
Fuck. You ruined everything!

2:44 a.m.
When did you stop loving me? Why did you stop loving me?

leaves voicemail
"Please wake up and call me back."

2:50 a.m.
I know you're sleeping beside her tonight. Did you bite her ear while spooning her as a way of saying goodnight like you used to do with me?
2:51 a.m.
I need you, please come back.
2:54 a.m.
WHY DO MY PILLOWS STILL SMELL OF YOU?

A Trail of Every Place I Have Ever Been

I smooth my skin over like a wrinkled map.
These palms tell stories of coursing rivers and
Crumbling mountains. My fingertips have become
Breadcrumbs, leaving a trail of every place I have ever
been.

Places where the sky has been a masterpiece.
Where orange and purple chased each other into
outstretched clouds.
Places where newly bloomed sunflowers competed for the
sun's attention.
Places where the ocean sang sweet symphonies to the
moon night after night.
Places where you touched my soul for the first time.

And though I have been
To the most breathtaking destinations,
I have also been to places where
My ribs became an earthquake,
Shattering the homes
In the city built in my lungs.

Places where colors fade and clouds rumble.
Places where the sun turns its back on those in need of
warmth,
Allowing them to die before they could even live.
Places where the ocean howls to the moon,
Begging her lover to return each morning before he leaves.
Places where you touched my soul for the last time.

I realized some of the prettiest places
Are also the most destructive.
So I will pinpoint the danger zones on my map,
And I will stay far away from them.

Moving On

I'm sorry that it took me so long to realize
That you are not my cure.
You're just everything that kills me,
And I unapologetically let you
Every time
Because I always thought that
That would somehow make you love me.
But you never will,
And I need to stop pretending otherwise.

Museum

He told me I was like a museum—intriguing and fascinating. The longer you stayed, the more you became interested. The longer you stayed, the more you learned. You learned why I was such a quiet place. Why people come and go, often without the slightest mutter. The only audible thing being a slight "hm" caught in the throat of visitors, and for some reason that was the only place it could stay for it never reached far enough to touch their lips.

He told me things about me, but I already knew them; I know that people come and go. I told him if he could hear the things that my heart hears, he would realize that I am not a museum. I'm not a place of beautifully hung art or impressive history. In fact, I am quite the opposite. I am a place that you never want to learn about. I do not withhold breathtaking pieces of ancient artifacts. I am not somewhere that people take their children or find love.

I am a haunted house. These ribs are the walls, the creaking stairs are my lungs. The echoes of this ghostly heartbeat fill my hollow chest. Many have entered in hopes of restoring this deadened soul—this living graveyard—but they all leave as zombies after too many sleepless nights. I drained them all.

You are intrigued now, but after a while you will soon become bored, wishing your departure could arrive sooner. Leaving me and texting your friends: "Sorry I didn't respond; I was at a stupid museum."

Birthmarks

My favorite things about you
Are all the ones you loathe
With your entire being.

The off-centered smile that hangs like the
Crescent moon.
The booming laugh that echoes in the loudest
Of rooms.
And the conspicuous birthmark that stains the
Left side of your chest.

The story goes that birthmarks
Often hint at how you died
In your previous life.
When I hear that,
I cannot help but think
Of how that dark smudge
Lingers over your heart

Did you die of
A broken heart?

And when you tell me
That I am your soulmate—
Always have been and
Always will be,
Was it me?

Did you know that
I am at fault?
Have you been
softly hinting at it?

If we retraced our steps
Back in time,
Into lives we once lived,
But have long forgotten,
Will we see that I am
Not just your lover,
But also your murderer?

Perhaps your wild heart
Knew that we would be
Together once again,
So you bear your mark
Like armor.
Like a shield against me,
Hoping that it will work
This time,
In this life.

BATTLES

Delightful Violence

Sometimes I am deep wine red,
A glass of champagne on a calm spring evening.
I am a slow dance and slight chuckles through smiling teeth.

But other times I am cracked lightning blue,
A finished bottle of vodka on a chilling winter night.
I am a tsunami and high-pitched screams muffled by pillows.

I am a dandelion in the summer, drifting atop the warm breeze.
I am a thorn on the stem of a beautiful rose.
I am fuzzy pajamas and fresh coffee in the morning.
I am broken glass and hole-punched walls.

My mind is both peaceful and violent all at once,
And I am still trying to figure out how.

Part 1: The Coward

I wear his hands like my favorite necklace,
Clasping so tightly around my throat
That I can taste my own heartbeat.
It tastes of cowardice and bad decisions.

My friends think that this is love,
That he just takes my breath away.
They cannot see that I am only breathless
Because I have learned to survive without oxygen.
I've learned how to hold onto the fading molecules
Until my vision becomes an obscured pointillism painted before me.

My friends think that this is love,
That he just can't keep his hands off me.
That's the problem—they think he touches out of adoration,
But he lays his hands on me to remind me that I belong to him.
The violet discoloration beneath my weary eyes screams so.

In Which I Fear That I Am Not Me Without My Illness

Sometimes I do not know
If I truly want to recover.
I have become so comfortable
In my sadness,
In my loneliness,
That I am afraid to live without it.
I have been this way for so long,
Will I still be me if I got better?

To the Men Who Love My Mouth

Men tell me that I look like
I know how to use my mouth,
That I must use it a lot.

They ask me what
I like to do with it,
As if it is a party trick.

This mouth is used
For speaking up;
For spitting venom on men
Who stare too long.

It refuses to clench around
Unwelcomed comments,
Gulping them down,
And digesting them
Like a normal meal.

This mouth is a feminist.

She is all rage and tantrums.
She is drunken fistfights
In a 4 a.m. parking lot.
She is the part of me
I wish I could be
At all times.

How I wish I were
As brave as she.
How I wish I were
As careless as she.

Just enough to stand up, but
I am afraid that if I did,
I would only be pushed back down.
I am afraid that if I did,
Everyone will realize that
I have been sitting the entire time.

So instead,
I stay in my seat,
Choke back the poison
As it mixes with their
Silver platter words, and
I thank them for the
Compliment.

A Letter to My Depression

I am not a rehabilitation center for a broken
promise like you.
Do not pry open my rib cage like the gates of an
abandoned hospital.
Do not climb inside and use this tomb to recover
and thrive.
Do not use my veins as your IV, soaking up all
the life that flows in my blood.

I am not your savior.
Do not slam your knees to the ground,
mold your hands together, and pray to me;
I will not save you.
I will not save you.

I am still trying to save me.

Detonate

My therapist once told me that
I am a safe full of grenades.
That I do not open up.
That it is impossible to get me to do so.
That one day the locked door will finally open,
and I will not be able to stop the explosion.

I feel the pins slowly slipping
with each passing day.
I am ticking from the inside out and
I hope that there is not a soul around
When I detonate.

No Means Yes

When a boy tried pulling on the hem of my baggy t-shirt,
I screamed no,
But I think my body was speaking
A language that I had never learned
Because he did not listen to my mouth.

Instead, he forced it closed,
Made me swallow my consent,
And took what he wanted.

My body is not my body,
I am just an object—
A pretty trinket for the taking.

I am just a badge on your trophy shelf,
A notch in your belt,
A story to brag about to your friends.
My humanity means nothing to you.

I wonder:
Do you ever think about it?
Does the memory replay in your head
Like a skipping record,
The only sound present is the
Guilt growing inside of you?

Or do you feel a sense of pride?
A warmth hugging you from the inside
Whenever you recall that day,

The only trophy left to cherish
Is the echoing of my tears?

I screamed no,
But maybe all you heard
Was a challenge.

I screamed no,
So why did you hear me
Whisper yes?

Part 2: He

He looks at me the way you look
At a plot of land that needs to be renovated.
He owns me but wants to change everything about me.
I let him.

I let him because I need him.
Because he reminds me every day
That no one else would ever love me.
That I should be thankful that he took it upon himself to do so.
As if he is a martyr.

Becoming A Ghost: A Magic Show

I watch my skin slowly disintegrate
Around my skeleton,
Becoming paper wrapped on porcelain bones.
I am disappearing,
But all they see is a success story.

Triggers

Trigger Warning:
Doctor's offices,
Action movies,
Men,
Mirrors.

Trigger
I do not know who I am anymore
Trigger
I do not know how to find me

How do you find yourself when
You are not sure where you lost yourself?
When you are not sure that
You are even lost?

I hide behind my own shadow
Trigger
Because I don't want people to know me
Trigger
Then complain that no one knows me

I am my own trigger
Every breath
Trigger
Every blink
Trigger
Every thought

Trigger
Trigger
Trigger

I wish that everything came
With a label
A warning
A "do you wish to continue" button

I do not know who I am
Trigger
I do not know who I will be
Trigger
But I hope
Trigger
To wake up one morning
And not think of pulling the
Trigger

Becoming Strangers

When a friend kissed me
Like it could save him,
He justified it,
Saying that it was okay because
I knew him.
Saying that I should be glad
It was him and not some stranger.
But what is the difference
When someone you know
Becomes someone
You thought you knew?

What If

What if I stopped breathing today?
What if I closed my eyes,
Let darkness in,
Gave him a cup of tea,
And offered him a seat on my couch?

What if every noise faded out,
Starting with my thumping heart,
Echoing its last concert in my
Auditorium chest?

The world will still spin,
Children will still laugh,
The sun will still die for the moon
Each day,
And life will carry on without me.

Forgive Me

I forgot to put my smile
On the charger last night.
I woke up this morning and
Forgot to polish my eyes so they gleam.
I didn't write happy on my calendar today
Because I am not.

So forgive me if the
Wind-up key on my back needs
A few extra turns to keep me going.

If I need to oil my
Rusted bones.

If my eyes do a cartwheel whenever
Someone lets ignorance spill from their mouth
Like a tipped paint can.

Forgive me if
I forget to act
Okay.

Do Not Ask Me What's Wrong

Because I know that I am
Vulnerable enough
To let you in;
To tell you my life story.
To think that you
Would actually care.

Part 3: Bruised Canvas

"No one will ever love you," he repeats.
I cannot help but to believe him as I stare at this body in the mirror.
This body that is littered in purple and brown patches of watercolor
That sit on display like I am a museum.

I lay them all in a row,
Each with its own plaque, stating the artist's inspirations.
This one is from two weeks ago,
When I neglected to answer the phone while out with friends.
This one is from last night,
When my trembling hands slipped from his mug,
Shattering it like my fragile bones.

It's funny;
I looked at the remnants
And only saw me reflected in them.

It's funny;
He claims he loves me,
But I have a better relationship with the coffee table
that catches me when my lover
Has had too much to drink at night.

How to Make a Bad Day Worse

First, convince yourself to get out of bed; that it will be worth it. Go to the bathroom and look at yourself in the mirror. Scan over your weary eyes and the lilac circles that lie beneath them. And even though they are hollowed from the pain, smile. Smile until it is convincing enough to say "I am fine" without breaking down again. Smile until it hurts, training your cheeks to stay where they should be. When you're finished, go to your loved one. Use your façade, look into their eyes, and secretly hope that they can see the truth in yours.

Next, enjoy breakfast together. Make some small talk. Go shopping together, run some errands. Have fun. Then, feel yourself numb as the pain slowly creeps its way back in. Take the smallest disagreement and make it an argument. Give each other the silent treatment.

He doesn't realize it, but he is your everything. All you really want is for him to grab you and hold you tight and tell you that you are his too. He doesn't. His pride will just let you cripple into nothing.

Cry in silence until you can no longer produce the tears. And because you are the weak one, apologize, even if you don't feel like you should. Hug him and lay beside him. Lay there until he is sleeping. Listen to his heavy breaths and think of all the reasons you fell in love with him.

Remember until your eyes are lead and your heart is full. Fall asleep with the hope that things will be different tomorrow.

Press repeat.

The Edge

I feel myself on the brink of relapse.
So close to the cliff's edge,
Every molecule in my body
Holds its own breath,
Afraid that one too deep may
Cause disaster.
I am scared.
I know that if I dive forward,
This small piece of sanity holding me
May snap,
Sending me further into a canyon
That I have spent years climbing out of.
But I don't know if I would be strong enough
To scale the walls this time.

I'm Sorry I Always Ask if You're Okay

I think I do it because
When I was breaking on the inside,
No one ever cared enough
To ask me the same.

The First Cut

It stings. It stings and seers as the pain radiates around the afflicted area. The edges welt into small, irritated hills on smooth skin and turn ghostly white. The only color evident is the center—a string of pink rises to the surface, decorated with small red pearls between shallow slits. For a second, it captivates you. Holds your hand and makes you forget why you came. But it does not matter. The pain is still there. The pain still spreads. You leave with a heavier heart than you brought in.

A Friend Long Forgotten

The thing about eating disorders
Is that you never fully recover.
I went from passing up food at gatherings
To people passing me their leftovers
And hit repeat.

Somehow, I am back where I started,
Miserable and disgusted with myself.

And though I gave Anorexia
Her friendship bracelet back years ago,
I still think of her from time to time.
I want to text her and ask how she's been.

I want to tell her that sometimes
I still look up if there are
Any calories present when
I lick my lips.

A Cursed House

I am but a cursed house.

My mind is the attic where
Broken windows allow
For bats to take shelter.
They hang upside down and
Sing high-pitched songs in my head.

My mouth, the entryway.
My heart, the ghost and
My soul is the wandering monster that
Scratches at the walls,
Trying to escape this pit of hell.

They say the eyes are
The windows to the soul,
So why can't you see
I am dead and haunted?

Why can't you see that
I wanted to be a suburban home
Where families move in,
That I wanted the green grass and
Children playing in the yard?

I wanted the love that
Kept this foundation together.

Why can't you see that
I am nothing more than
a cursed house?

It's Getting Bad Again

I can't get out of bed,
Or out of my head.
All these thoughts I am having
Make me wish I was dead.

This Will Make Me Feel Pretty

My bedside table is littered with diet pills
And empty bottles of water.
Pride tastes better than any food
I have ever eaten.

I watch myself pretend
I am not hungry and then
Hunch over the toilet,
Trying to spit out my extra weight.

I am sick. I know that I am sick.
But I also know that this
Will make me feel pretty.
So I avoid pitying eyes and lunch.
I wear tighter clothes to make me
Aware of my body,
Maybe then I will push myself harder.

This is not an instruction manual,
But a cry for help.
This is me begging to silence
The calculator in my head
Whenever I think about dinner.

This is me asking my body for
Forgiveness.

Coming Home

This is not a relapse.
It is like coming home after
Being away for so long.

Excuse Me

I have tried to kill the demons that possess this body several times. So excuse me if I am annoyed by the boy in my bio lecture who jokes of suicide when given an extra assignment. I've had bruises in the shape of a strong hand lay claim to my arm when I didn't thank the man attached to it for telling me what he would like to do to me. So excuse me for gritting my teeth and making rockets of my feet when walking past men. I have been the butt of the joke, felt the punchline snarl its sharp teeth at me. So now I refuse to keep silent and ignore the mockery. I will not apologize for being serious about serious matters. I know you look at my girlish figure, bright eyes, and long hair and just see a pleasant spring day. I am anything but. I am fire and rage and white knuckles on clenched fists. I am standing up because somebody has to. Because I am tired of being brushed off like loose dirt. I am tired of swallowing pieces of my teeth, chipped from biting away the courage to change the world. So excuse me if I let it slip past my crooked smile and fall to the floor. Excuse me if I say more than you wanted to hear; I am just tired of being silent.

Truce

I will never truly know
If I have the potential to love
This body.
I will never truly know
If I could ever be happy
In this body.

I have spent so many years
Raging war on this castle of flesh and bone,
I do not know how to call it truce.
I do not know how to raise my white flag,
But I am trying.

Body, forgive me.
I am trying.

Beautifully Imperfect

Sometimes when we cuddle,
The rumbling of my lover's stomach
Sends earthquakes into my spine;
A vibration strong enough to
Echo off my bones and ring in the
Abandoned cage of my chest.

Sometimes he would rather
Go to bed hungry than
Without his clothes on.
Sometimes I ache to find
The words to describe just how
Beautiful his body is to me.

How every time he does
Find the confidence to
Strip down to his skin and
Bare his soul,
I cannot help but to
Marvel at the sight.

How I wish to trace
Every ghost of a scar,
Every evidence of a stretch mark,
Every constellation of imperfection.

How I wish to tell him that
He is perfect with all his flaws
And have him believe it too.

Yellow Paint

Vincent Van Gogh had a tortured mind. For example, he used to eat yellow paint during episodes of depression and paralyzing anxiety. People usually mistake this for him believing it would make him happy again. In fact, Van Gogh knew it was bad for him and tried eating it to slowly poison himself. He consumed it to numb and kill the pain he felt. This set him on the road to self-destruction and suicidal tendencies.[3]

I believe that we all, in some way, have our own yellow paint. Something that slowly but completely tears us apart. It drives us mad from the inside out. Maybe it is a thing, a place, or even a person. Maybe it is a memory that you cannot seem to escape, reliving it over and over.

We have our own poisons—our own cyanide and turpentine. And sometimes we do not realize that they are killing us until it is too late.

---

[3] "Did Van Gogh Eat Yellow Paint?" Van Gogh Museum, accessed September 27, 2020.

Shrink

Two lamps softly illuminate Freudian posters that hang on dim walls. I sit on a couch that smells faintly of my grandmother—a thought that makes me more afraid to let the secrets spill from my mouth like an overflowing sink. Afraid that wherever she is, her ears will hear it and her heart will ache—a stain that cannot be fully removed. It is not a sturdy couch. Perhaps the years of eavesdropping on countless heavy souls and trying to be strong enough to hold them up when they are breaking down, has worn its wooden bones into splinters. He sits across from me with soft eyes and crossed legs, asks me to speak but all I have learned is how to turn my stubborn mouth into a kitchen. I talked my trauma into a meal and when I feel I have said too much, I pack up the leftovers and hide them in the cupboard of my throat so no one else can have a taste. I wash it down with the tears that I have been too numb to cry. A feast which fills me. Oh, to be so full, yet still so empty within.

RECOVERY

Part 4: Healing

It's been three years since I left. My new lover does not touch me without asking, afraid that I might recoil into myself. Afraid that I am a trigger finger, and the smallest movement will set this gun off. He is gentle with me, reminding me that I am never at fault—that he will be there to help heal my broken parts. He leaves me breathless, then breathes the air back into me. He looks at me like a newly built dream home, one that you can see your whole life in, one that you are proud to have. He leaves kisses on my museum skin and he catches me when I have had too much to drink.

I Am

I am worth more than this
I am more than empty pill bottles,
Tear-stained pillows,
And broken mirrors.

I am beauty and love;
I am sunshine and flowers;
I am joy.

I am worthy of happiness.

Recovering

I am a work in progress.
I still have so far to go,
but I am proud of how far I have come.

The Beauty in Life

White-capped ocean waves that roar louder than lions and
Violently swallow sandcastles.
Diamond-dusted stars that collide into a colorful firework show and
Create new galaxies beyond.
Dew-tipped blades of grass that salute the sun and
Slice the gentle breeze as it passes by.

Life is so beautiful, and I hope that
You wake in the morning to
See it for yourself.

Today Is A New Day

I wore your favorite color today,
but I did not cry.
I listened to our song today,
but I did not think of you singing it.
I drove past your house today,
but I did not glance back.
I do not think about you as much as I used to.
I still get sad that you left me,
But it does not hurt like it did before today.

What If (Cont'd)

But what if I stayed alive?
What if I closed my eyes,
Counted to ten,
And kept going?

What if I stopped calling
It "noise" and started calling
It "music" instead?

The world will still spin,
Children will still laugh,
The sun will still die for the moon
Each day,
And life will carry on with me.

But it will be so much prettier
To live.
To see the years spin by.
To one day hear my own children laugh.
To see the sun and moon live out their romance.
To carry on.

5 Words You Should Hear

I am proud of you.

The Road to Recovery

Growth is not always constant.
Some days will feel as still as a shuffled playlist
Full of the same, tired song.
Other days will feel like you are
Walking backwards through
A Boston Marathon.

But you will have good days.
Days where development is evident
And smiles are genuine.
The road to recovery is
Long and winding,
Full of obstacles and setbacks.

Do not let them
Undermine your
Progress.

Giving Up

Giving up would make the most sense right now.
Just let the cold take over again,
Instead of trying to fight it.
But I remember what it was like
To be lost in the dark,
What I was like.

I burned bridges
And bridges turned into cities.
I burned people who
Didn't deserve that;
I didn't deserve that.

Giving up would make the most sense right now,
But I have strong bones and a stubborn mind,
Gifts given to me
By my mother.
And it is time I learned
How to use them.

Baby Steps

I started baking again, today,
A favorite pastime that I lost
When sadness moved in.

I started singing again.
I watered my plants
And apologized for neglecting their needs.
I sat outside and enjoyed the warmth
Of the sun on my chilled skin.

I laughed at myself when I spilled flour,
Instead of crying and screaming
Of how much of an idiot I am.
I ate an extra cookie and I read on my couch.

I still dislike who I am,
But today,
I love myself more than I did
Yesterday.

Stardust

Rome wasn't built in a day,
And neither were you.
You were carefully stitched together
With stardust and imperfection.
Everything about you
Is beautiful.
Your constellation freckles,
Your river-eroded palms,
And your orchestra laugh.

Every day,
You continue to be molded into something
So extraordinary,
Despite the weathering of your shell.
Despite the times you
Have caved in on yourself.

You are ever more lovely
Than you believe yourself to be.
Oh, how I cannot wait until
You see it too.

To All the Boys

To the boys struggling with mental illnesses, abusive relationships, and eating disorders. To the boys who survived sexual assault and self-harming tendencies. To all the boys who have been told it is weak to show emotion, to be anything but stone cold. To all the boys who do not get the help they need because these things "don't happen to men." Keep fighting because you are strong enough to get through this and deserve to be seen.

Rain Bow

Maybe it is not pronounced "*rainbow*,"
But it is "*rain bow.*"

It can bring mighty storms to its knees.
Show that the rolling clouds
And flickering switches
Are not so scary after all.

Show that there will be calm
And light after all has passed.
That there is beauty in any storm
And happiness waits
On the other side.

Maybe we have underestimated
The power of beautiful
Things.

Process

Recovery is not to return
To how things used to be.
Recovery is not becoming your
Old self again and acting like nothing
Ever happened.
It is not all journaling,
Morning yoga,
And counting to ten when
You feel like breaking.
Recovery is a process.
A trial and error.
Recovery is learning that you have grown
And changed and cannot go back
To your old self.
It is growing in a different direction,
But still heading to the same destination.

Reminders in the Mirror: A Haiku

You're a good person,
You are worthy of good things,
And you are so loved.

Don't Look Back

Your future needs you, your past doesn't.

Meant to Be

I have found that I no longer
Have to burn
My skin to feel a fiery passion.
I have found one inside of myself
When I swallowed my
Battery acid smiles and prerecorded excuses.

I have found that the sun
Is not the only source of warmth,
But so is my laughter;
Soft and sweet,
Yet powerful enough to make others
Feel at home.

I have found that I can love
And be loved simultaneously,
And the world will not collapse
On top of me.
I can give pieces of me
Without destroying myself
And above all,
I can love myself wholeheartedly.
No complications,
No mistakes.

I have found that I
Am meant to be.

HOTLINES

According to the mental health awareness and suicide prevention website, Pleaselive.org, "hotlines have three things in common:

1) they are available to call 24/7
2) they are 100% confidential
3) they are free

This is a list of hotlines that can be helpful for any type of situation you may be in or struggling with."[4]

SUICIDE:

National Suicide Prevention Hotline:
   1-800-273-8255

Deaf Hotline:
   1-800-799-4889

EATING DISORDERS:

Eating Disorders Awareness and Prevention:
   1-800-931-2237

---

4   "List of Hotlines." 2010. Please Live. Davo Productions, accessed November 11, 2020.

Eating Disorders Center:
1-888-236-1188

National Association of Anorexia Nervosa and Associated Disorders:
1-847-831-3438

ABUSE AND DOMESTIC VIOLENCE:
National Sexual Assault Hotline:
1-800-656-4673

National Domestic Violence Hotline:
1-800-799-7233

National Domestic Violence Hotline Spanish:
1-800-942-6908

National Child Abuse Hotline:
1-800-4-A-CHILD (422-4453)

Child Abuse Hotline / Dept. of Social Services:
1-800-342-3720

Rape, Abuse, and Incest National Network (RAINN):
1-800-656-HOPE (4673)

LGBTQIA+:
Helpline:
1-800-398-4297

Gay and Lesbian National Hotline:
1-888-843-4564

Trevor Project Hotline (Suicide):
1-866-488-7386

ADDICTION:
Alcohol Treatment Referral Hotline (24 hours):
1-800-252-6465

Families Anonymous:
1-800-736-9805

Drug Abuse National Helpline:
1-800-662-4357

National Association for Children of Alcoholics:
1-800-662-4357

Alcoholics for Christ:
1-800-441-7877

SELF-INJURY:
S.A.F.E. (Self Abuse Finally Ends):
1-800-DONT-CUT (366-8288)

CRISIS:
(Under 18)

Girls and Boys Town:
1-800-448-3000

Hearing Impaired:
1-800-448-1833

Youth Crisis Hotline:
1-800-448-4663

Teen Hope Line:
1-800-394-HOPE (4673)

(Any age)

United Way Crisis Helpline:
1-800-233-HELP (4357)

Christian Oriented Hotline:
1-877-949-HELP (4357)

Social Security Administration:
1-800-772-1213

ACKNOWLEDGEMENTS

I cannot express enough how grateful I am to have been able to write this book. It has always been a dream of mine, and it is unfathomable to think that it has come true. I want to give an incredibly special thanks to each and every person who has been a part of *Trigger Warning*. Everyone who opened up to me because of it. Everyone who stood beside me. Everyone who supported my writing from the beginning, way before a book was ever a thought. Everyone who had a hand in making this a reality. From the bottom of my heart, a simple thank you will never be enough:

Sandra Beck, Terry Bergren, Sheena Cunningham, Tammy Darwin, Jordan Doegg, Lauren Fager, Kendall Helton, Ashlee Horne, Amber Hulsey, Brianna Johnekins, Gavin Jones, Eric Koester, Teresa Lovell, Cassondra Nanoff, Brianna Plancher, Ashlee Runyon, Pluto Sheridan, Torrie Southern, Tania Stiers, Kerrick Taggart, Rachael Tate, NickI Thompson, Cody Turner, Jade Waughtel, Brianna Webb, and Antoin Zaher.

I would also like to give a shoutout to fellow authors Breanna Decker, Grant Dever, Amy Dong, Bailee Noella, Lauren Stikeleather, and Julia Weidman, and to my friends and family—Tammy Darwin, Teresa Lovell, Cassondra Nanoff, Kerrick Taggart, Rachael Tate, and Jade Waughtel—for the praise that they have given to *Trigger Warning*.

Lastly, I would like to thank Professor Eric Koester along with New Degree Press for giving me this opportunity, including Brian Bies, Clayton Bohle, Elina Oliferovskiy, Leila Summers, and everyone else who dedicated their time to making sure this book gets out into the world. I appreciate everything you all have done for me.

APPENDIX

FHE Health. "Statistics on Mental Trauma." Addiction & Mental Health Care. Accessed October 26, 2020. fherehab.com/trauma/statistics.

Torres, Felix. "What Is Depression?" American Psychiatric Association, Accessed on October 26, 2020. https://www.psychiatry.org/patients-families/depression/what-is-depression.

"Did Van Gogh Eat Yellow Paint Thinking That It Would Raise His Spirits?" Accessed September 27, 2020. https://www.vangoghmuseum.nl/en/art-and-stories/vincent-van-gogh-faq/did-van-gogh-eat-yellow-paint.

"List of Hotlines." 2010. Please Live. Davo Productions. Accessed November 11, 2020. http://www.pleaselive.org/hotlines/.

www.ingramcontent.com/pod-product-compliance
Lightning Source LLC
LaVergne TN
LVHW011845060526
838200LV00054B/4178